Débora de Lima Marreiro

Integral Education

Débora de Lima Marreiro

Integral Education

the importance of evaluation and monitoring

ScienciaScripts

Publisher:
Sciencia Scripts
is a trademark of
Dodo Books Indian Ocean Ltd. and OmniScriptum S.R.L publishing group

120 High Road, East Finchley, London, N2 9ED, United Kingdom
Str. Armeneasca 28/1, office 1, Chisinau MD-2012, Republic of Moldova, Europe
Printed at: see last page
ISBN: 978-620-7-74810-5

SUMMARY

"To educate is to educate oneself in the practice of freedom, it is the task of those who know that they know little - so they know something and can thus come to know more - in dialogue with those who almost always think they know nothing, so that the latter, by transforming their thinking that they know nothing into knowing that they know little, can also know more."

Paulo Freire

DEDICATORY

I dedicate my research to my husband and work partner, Edcarlos Ferreira, who accepted the great challenge of coordinating Integral Education alongside me.

To my children and grandchildren who inspire me to contribute to social transformation through education.

To my friend Vânia Bernal, who guided me during my research and data organization.

INTRODUCTION

"Education, the right of all and the duty of the State and the family, shall be promoted and encouraged with the collaboration of society, aiming at the full development of the person, their preparation for the exercise of citizenship and their qualification for work". (Art. 205, Federal Constitution)

Thinking about the proposal to implement a Full-Time Education Program implies understanding how the process of articulating academic and community groups, implementing, evaluating and monitoring a public policy on full-time education is carried out, with the aim of establishing strategies that allow us to understand what the difficulties are and how to overcome them, so that management practices can guarantee a voice for the participants in the process.

It also requires thinking about the school day according to a concept of integral education, which advocates not only extending the time spent at school or in educational spaces, but which has a perspective that represents the expansion of significant learning opportunities that boost autonomy and the development of critical thinking.

It is worth taking a closer look at the concepts used in this research when referring to "integral education" and "full-time school", as set out by Ana Cavaliere and Jaqueline Moll.

Integral education - Educational action that involves diverse and wide-ranging dimensions of individual formation. When associated with non-intentional education, it refers to the broad socializing and formative processes that are practiced by all societies, through all their actors and actions, and is a necessary consequence of the coexistence between adults and children. [...] When it refers to school education, it has the sense of a connection between the intentional action of the school institution and life in the broadest sense. (CAVALIERE, 2010, p. 39)

Full-time school - In a narrow sense, this refers to school organization in which students' time is extended beyond the school day, also known in some countries as the full school day. In a broad sense, it encompasses the debate on comprehensive education - taking into account formative needs in the cognitive, aesthetic, ethical, recreational, physical-motor and spiritual fields, among others - in which the category of "school time" has an important significance both in terms of its expansion and the need to reinvent it in everyday school life. (MOLL, 2010, p. 39)

Full-time education is directly related to affirmative action policies, prioritizing social classes that have historically been excluded or vulnerable. Full-time education often has a shelter-related purpose, removing children from the street.

The study presented in this research, carried out in the municipality of Santos/SP, reports on an experience that portrayed the implementation of a new evaluation and monitoring model that considered the different dimensions and various participants in the process, involving students, educators and parents.

The proposed evaluation, focusing on the educational aspect of Integral Education, considered the limited theoretical foundation available and the theoretical proposal that underpins the Program under study, based on the Four Pillars of Education, proposed by Jacques Delors.

Understanding the Four Pillars of Education: Learning to be, learning to learn, learning to do and learning to live together, underpins the conceptual approach used as a backdrop to the design and implementation of the evaluation and monitoring of the Comprehensive Education program.

Implementing comprehensive education policies implies making a commitment to education that goes beyond the idea of extending the time spent at school and aims to fulfill the social function of giving future generations access to historically accumulated knowledge through different languages, contributing to the expansion of existing symbolic capital, giving students the chance to get to know the world in which they live, understand its contradictions and encourage themselves to make decisions in a true exercise of autonomy and citizenship, as Hanna Arendt argues when she states that:

> Education is the point at which we decide whether we love the world enough to take responsibility for it and, with such a gesture, save it from the ruin that would be inevitable were it not for renewal and the arrival of the new and the young. Education is also where (sic) we decide whether we love our children enough not to expel them from our world and abandon them to their own resources, nor to snatch from their hands the opportunity to undertake something new and unforeseen for us, but instead to prepare them in advance for the task of renewing a common world. (ARENDT, 1979, p. 247).

The research presented in this study refers to comprehensive education in the municipality of Santos/SP, during changes in the evaluation and monitoring proposal in 2013, when the Comprehensive Education Program, called Total School, served approximately 4.376 students in Nùcleos (spaces dedicated to pedagogical, sporting and cultural activities in the period immediately opposite regular education) and in full-time Municipal Education Units, in addition to the 930 students taking part in the Para Ver a Banda Tocar (To See the Band Play) Project, which develops band and flute activities.

In an analysis of the data available from the program's implementation in 2006 until 2012, it was noticed that only the children's learning was used for monitoring and evaluation purposes. However, it was considered that other dimensions would also need to be monitored in order to increase the quality of comprehensive education, respecting different perspectives and analyzing opinions in different areas.

In 2013, with the change in municipal management, the new coordinators of the Total School Program implemented some changes: the insertion of the function of Specific Coordinators (which promoted greater dialogue with the technical teams of the Municipal Education Units), the work with projects in the axes of art and pedagogical orientation, the specificity of the projects for the martial arts area, the studies of the environment planned with formative dimensions for the educators, who would later develop them with the students, in addition to the training of the educators according to the specificities of the workshops carried out.

Another interesting factor is that the program has always aimed to increase the number of people served, and in order to increase this number with the desired quality, it is necessary to have a policy of continuous evaluation and monitoring of the work. The monitoring previously carried out relied on an external consultancy, but since 2013 it has not been possible to continue, which has made it possible to draw up an evaluation and monitoring matrix proposed by people directly involved in the whole process.

Therefore, some relevant points were considered for the evaluation and monitoring of the program, reflecting both structural and pedagogical dimensions.

The following dimensions were evaluated:

a)   Articulation of the program in the territory and in the city;

b)   Training educators;

c)   Infrastructure and material conditions;

d)   Access and permanence;

e)   Educational practices.

Based on some indicators drawn up by the program's coordinators and pedagogical guidance team for each of these dimensions, some strategies were chosen and data collection instruments were developed to enable reliable analysis. In the following chapters, we will analyze the results based on the data collected in the light of the available bibliography that underpins the discussion.

1   EVALUATION IN INTEGRAL EDUCATION

In Brazil, since the Federal Constitution, there have been references to the idea of Integral Education and the integral formation of individuals. In reference to formal education, LDB 9394/96, in its Article 34, encourages education systems to progressively extend the school day in primary education. The school day is considered to be the period in which children and adolescents are under the responsibility of the school, in in-school and/or out-of-school activities.

Nowadays, there are countless reasons why parents are looking to extend study time or the school day, which, in addition to enabling greater integration with other educational spaces that provide diversified educational practices, in an intentional action, reassures parents in the sense of guaranteeing security for their children in a greater space and time spent in the school environment.

In order to understand the dimensions that make it possible to analyze the effectiveness of extending time, some factors and reasons will be discussed, such as evaluation in a Comprehensive Education Program.

Formal evaluation has always been advocated in education, but the scarcity of bibliography on evaluation with regard to different languages is still a major challenge for new evaluation cultures and practices.

> The results of learning assessments and the conditions of this learning in contexts of social vulnerability are indicators of the demands for universality in educational policy. We reiterate that these conditions form an integral part of the conditions of choice regarding participation in full-time education, on the part of the students and their families. In this sense, the parameters of choice are objective and are not restricted to idiosyncrasies, will, desire or refusal as to whether or not to participate in full-time education (MOLL, 2012, p. 44).

Thinking about the collective construction of an Integral Education Program implies understanding how the process of collective participation and the articulation of academic and community knowledge takes place in an implementation proposal that guarantees evaluation and monitoring in the search for quality in integral education.

It is worth highlighting Paro's contributions when he states that:

> There is a tendency to think that extending schooling time is just that: doing in more time what is already being done today. This can be extremely dangerous because we could simply be adding to the misery, giving more of the same thing. We don't want to think only of full-time education as a banner of struggle, but to articulate this extension with a concept of comprehensive education, [...] after all, what education do we want to

If developing an evaluation that is coherent with the concept of Integral Education adopted by the municipality is a challenge, on the other hand, starting from a concept based on the precepts of Jacques Delors provides a theoretical foundation that guides the vision of monitoring as a way of implementing Integral Education that fulfills its role of providing participating students with another, extended education.

When considering the historical perspective, as an institutional experience, the proposal for evaluating and monitoring full-time full-time education should take into account various aspects that aim to broaden knowledge, curricula and learning; consider the subjects, knowledge, times and spaces of learning; highlight autonomy in decision-making and the implementation of actions that enhance comprehensive education as a subject's right; intensify the relationship between the community and educational spaces in the perspective of the Educating City.

From this perspective, Paulo Freire states that:

A school is not just a physical space. It's a working environment, an attitude, a way of being". This is why we believe that schools, whether full-time or not, should be schools of "integral education", which encourage the expansion and diversity of learning experiences, the circulation around the greatest number of diversified learning environments, and which contribute to the construction of the longed-for autonomy [...] (FREIRE, 1991, p. 16).

And why isn't full-time education for all students a reality in Santos and in Brazil? The number of schools in Brazil is only sufficient because students spend part of their day at school, because if the Brazilian school day were full time (morning and afternoon) the shortage of schools and professionals would be evident. In countries where the school day is extended to six or eight hours a day, there is greater proficiency, which can be seen, for example, in the Program for International Student Assessment (PISA) of the Organization for Economic Cooperation and Development (OECD).

PISA and other institutional assessments have their value and importance in the cognitive sphere, but when it comes to assessment from the perspective of integral development, there is a lack of information on "how to assess socio-emotional competences". All the material available reinforces the idea that assessment is an inherent part of the educational process, but when we researched assessment proposals with a view to multiple languages, the challenge was to innovate and create an instrument that would meet the needs and objectives of the Comprehensive Education Program in the municipality of Santos.

As with all research, we wanted to "drink" from academic sources that indicated a route that had already been taken, so that we could adapt it to the reality of the program's participants. Faced with the difficulty of finding good examples available for consultation and study, we came up with the well-known "Big Five" and will explain below the route taken to develop an instrument that is coherent with the concept of Integral Education that underpins the research.

1.1   The challenge of building an evaluation tool

The need to evaluate is inherent in the educational process, as stated above, but the evaluation of projects and programs has been built in Brazil based on good international examples. We cite PISA as one of the large-scale evaluations that has been the subject of heated debate, sparking discussions about human development, schooling, learning and evaluation procedures.

In Brazil, some initiatives such as the Ayrton Senna Institute's proposal, in partnership with the Organization for Economic Cooperation and Development (OECD), propose measuring socio-emotional competencies in students from the 5th year of elementary school to the 3rd year of secondary school.

Researching and trying to understand human learning and development implies looking for strategies and possibilities for assessing this learning. When it comes to integral development, in the social and emotional spheres, ensuring that cognitive, physical and cultural aspects are addressed, the challenge becomes immeasurable.

On this path, during the research for the development of the evaluation tool, we found two references that supported the choice adopted by the Municipal Program in Santos from 2013 to 2016: the proposal for a mandala view of education, which guarantees a look at singularity in harmony with plurality, and the proposal called Social and Emotional Non-cognitive Nationwide Assessment (SENNA).

The SENNA Project is based on the idea that:

> [...] skills and abilities such as perseverance, autonomy and curiosity are just as important as cognitive skills (measured by performance tests and IQ) for achieving good results in various spheres of individual and collective well-being, such as education, income and health. More than that: the evidence suggests that these skills benefit outcomes in adult life via schooling, i.e. through their contribution to school success. (SANTOS; PRIMI, 2014, p. 5)

In a report entitled "Socio-emotional development and school learning: A measurement proposal to support public policies", written by Daniel Santos and Ricardo Primi (2014), the preliminary results of the above-mentioned project refer to a "[...] broad set of psychometric instruments established in international literature [...]" (SANTOS; PRIMI, 2014, p. 12). The authors also state that the project's first major objective was to build an instrument that was both "economically viable for large-scale application" and "scientifically robust to support academic research in the area".

All research must respect scientific rigor and the authors of SENNA refer to research conducted by economists, psychologists and educators and speak of the "rigorous vision" of the studies and the "positive impact proven by scientific evidence". They emphasize the relevance of socio-emotional development for learning and admit the importance of schools which, even though they are not currently prepared for the needs of the new times, still "[...] contribute to the development of socio-emotional attributes associated with success [...]." (SANTOS; PRIMI, 2014, p.15)

They also state that there is a consensus among psychologists that the most effective way of analyzing human personality is to observe it in five dimensions, known as the Big Five: Openness to New Experiences, Extraversion, Amiability, Conscientiousness and Emotional Stability, the Big Five.

The Big Five is a proposal based on responses to broad questionnaires with diverse questions about behaviors representative of numerous personality traits. When applied to people from different cultures and at different points in time, these questionnaires proved to have the same latent factor structure, giving rise to the "hypothesis that the personality traits of human beings are effectively grouped around five major domains". (SANTOS; PRIMI, 2014, p. 17)

The analysis carried out in this study revealed some questionable points in relation to the basis of the proposal, including the assertion that every individual should be analyzed in terms of the five personality dimensions described in the Big Five. In view of the above, readers may be wondering what crucial role the study of the Big Five played in the development of the assessment instrument proposed to the students participating in the program under analysis in this study. Let's just say that it was of great value in many respects, but mainly in relation to the importance of separating cognitive assessment from socio-emotional assessment and thinking about which dimensions should be assessed according to the theoretical matrix that underpins the Comprehensive Education program at municipal level.

With regard to the problem of thinking of an instrument that would assess cognitive and socio-emotional skills, the Big Five makes it explicit in the title of the proposal, and discards, as a matter of principle, the intrinsic relationship between emotion and cognition.

Faced with these difficulties, our proposal was to develop an instrument that encompassed the principles that govern mandalas, with the necessary symmetry and the Four Pillars of Education that form the theoretical foundation of the Integral Education proposal.

In general, education policies and practices are based on conceptions that are nourished by theories developed in different fields of knowledge such as psychology, philosophy and pedagogy. Following this path, the proposal for socio-emotional assessment was generated and put into practice from 2013 to 2016, under the coordination of the person responsible for the ongoing research.

2 EVALUATION AND MONITORING OF THE COMPREHENSIVE EDUCATION PROGRAM

"Education, the right of all and the duty of the State and the family, will be promoted and encouraged with the collaboration of society, aiming at the full development of the person, their preparation for the exercise of citizenship and their qualification for work". (Art. 205, Federal Constitution)

The evaluation and monitoring of the Comprehensive Education Program "Total School", instituted by Law No. 2394 of May 26, 2006, followed the format set out below from 2013 to 2016. Some changes were made to the proposals based on the results collected in the five dimensions used to evaluate the Program, as we will see below.

2. 1 Dimension: Articulation in the territory and the city

We promoted integration with federal programs, built some partnerships with public and private institutions and brought students closer to the city's learning spaces. This strategy stimulated the students' sense of belonging to the space they live in. In other words, this action aims to get the students to walk through the city's spaces feeling uninhibited and comfortable, enjoying them and at the same time understanding and apprehending the social values of each of the spaces they experience.

All the students in the program took part in different environmental studies, which involved visits to the Engenho dos Erasmos Ruins Monument and the Chico Mendes Botanical Garden, as well as a guided streetcar tour of the historic center. In each of these places, they acquired specific knowledge, values and attitudes that are important for civic life. Therefore, with a view to broadening the students' world view, we searched the city itself for spaces that favor the construction of knowledge in general.

During the period under study, other partnerships were established:

• Partnerships with the Federal Government: Programa Mais Educaçâo and Programa Segundo Tempo;

• Partnerships with civil society:

I. Papa Cartão Program - R. S. de Paula/Ecopere company to encourage the collection of cards that would otherwise be discarded in order to encourage environmentally conscious practices;

II. Raizes Project - partnership with Colégio Jean Piaget (Santos) encouraging planting and the construction of compost bins;

III.   The Tatiana Belink Reading Room at CAIS Milton Teixeira encourages reading and storytelling - donated by the Bunge Foundation;

IV.   SESC - Training in mini athletics to encourage sport based on different skills.

- Partnerships with Municipal Secretariats:

I.   Department of the Environment: Chico Mendes Botanical Garden, Municipal Orchid Garden.

II.   Tourist Office: Tram.

III.   Department of Culture: Municipal Theater, Portuguese Language Museum.

IV.   Sports Department: Roberto Mário Santini Park.

- Cultural partnerships:

I.   Donation of 950 children's books for the reading activities of the

II.   Total School Program (Municipal Education Council).

III.   Sol, Amigo da Infância (Brazilian Society of Dermatology/São Paulo state regional office).

IV.   Exhibition: "100 years of History and Energy" (CPFL partnership with the Ministry of Culture and support from the city council).

V.   Event: Peace Wave (Citizenship Secretariat/Total School).

VI.   *Non Violence* Project - Sport for Peace.

VII.   Projeto Leitores do Amanha (Sponsor: A Tribuna newspaper - relaunch of the A Tribuninha supplement).

All these links show how the program has allowed students to strengthen their ties with the neighborhood and the city in general.

2.2 Dimension: Training educators

In 2013, the program's coordinators created a pedagogical guidance team that was responsible for the ongoing training of all participating educators and also for monitoring and guiding the work carried out at the Municipal Full-Time Education Centers and Units.

The hubs are spaces close to the schools that receive students during the period opposite to regular school hours to carry out educational, sporting and cultural activities during the extended school day. Full-time schools allow students to take part in activities to extend the school day in the school itself.

Monthly training meetings were planned and carried out, respecting the specificities of each of the three areas of work provided for in the curriculum matrix in force during the period under study: arts, sports and pedagogical guidance.

Every year, the Arts team chose a theme that would generate awareness of other cultures and their incorporation into our daily lives. Through the training of art educators, the students were able to learn about and appreciate the cultural richness of the various artistic manifestations present in our daily lives: music, dance, rhythms, prints, colors, clothing, among other customs. The development of this work sought to broaden the aesthetic outlook as well as to give the students a repertoire of diversity.

The pedagogical axis training for the Pedagogical Experience/Hour of Duty educators focused on Reading and Writing Skills and Logical Reasoning. The Storytelling educators took part in work with literature that allowed them to use multiple languages both in the storytelling and in the pedagogical developments of their work with the students. Training to stimulate reading was constantly promoted for all the educators taking part in the different strands, as we believe that reading can be included in all the workshops, given its relevance to citizens' lives.

The implementation of the sports axis included sports and fighting/martial arts and led to a project that culminated in a gigantic presentation at the International Fighting Festival, which has now been incorporated into the municipality's social calendar given the scale of the proposal. At the Festival, all the workshops and axes were covered in their abilities and potential. Another important point was that, as it was a festival, all the students taking part were awarded prizes and the four types of fighting (karate, judo, capoeira and taekwondo) took place at the same time.

The training meetings were planned at the beginning of the year and the dates and objectives were made known to parents and guardians by means of a "Letter to Parents" (APPENDIX H) to facilitate family organization, since the extension of the school day was suspended at the monthly meeting. Parents were very supportive as they understood the importance of continuing training for community educators as an investment in the quality of comprehensive education.

So, after presenting an overview of how the educators' training was planned and carried out, we move on to evaluating this dimension.

Analyzing the results of the "EVALUATION OF EDUCATORS' TRAINING" (APPENDIX A), answered in groups by the coordinators of the Total School - Extended Day Program centers, represented by graph 1, we conclude that the number of training meetings from the point of view of the center coordinators, on a scale where 5 is the best evaluation, was satisfactory, because they scored between the best and the next best, that is, 5 and 4.

Graph 1 - Training evaluation

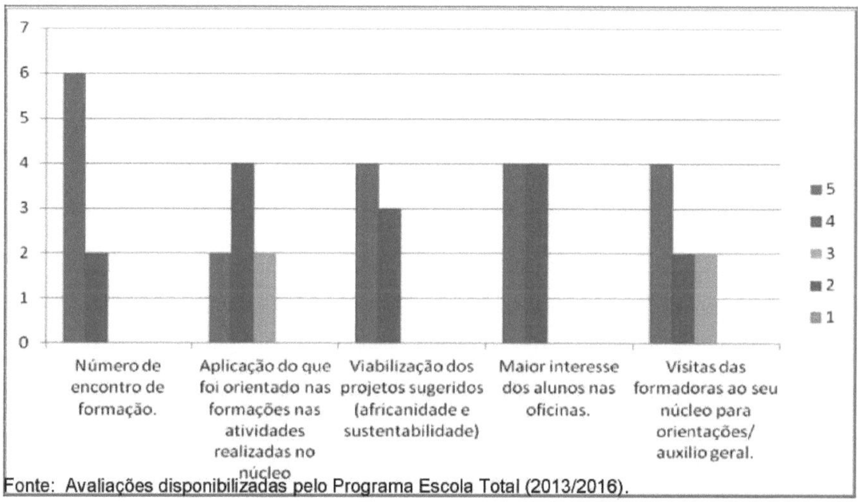

Fonte: Avaliações disponibilizadas pelo Programa Escola Total (2013/2016).

Regarding the question of what is oriented in the trainings and what is carried out by the educators in the centers, the scores were between 5, 4 and 3, so we see that this question should be observed as something to be improved, because we understand from this result that there are still educators who do not satisfactorily use what is proposed in the trainings.

When it came to making the suggested projects viable, they were rated between 5 and 4, and one group abstained from answering. We consider this to be an important success factor to be maintained: the work with projects in training courses achieved the expected result.

When asked about the students' interest in the workshop activities during the year, they scored 5 and 4, which shows that the training has achieved its objectives: to arouse greater student interest through challenging and meaningful activities.

Finally, the item referring to visits by trainers to the centers for guidance and general assistance was rated between 5 and 4, which also shows that visits are positive strategies for constantly improving the quality of the program.

We conclude that, in terms of ongoing training, the path we have traveled has been successful, with just one caveat regarding some of the practices carried out at the centers.

The training aims to promote the quality of the workshops, so the lesson plans should reflect what was oriented in the training meetings. This issue was monitored more closely by the trainers during subsequent visits to the centers.

It is worth noting that after the first evaluation carried out with core coordinators, in the following years the evaluations took place with the participation of each community educator working in the program.

2.3 Dimension: Infrastructure and material conditions

The infrastructure and material conditions were analyzed with reference to the following indicators: number of educators, sufficient space and quantity of materials for the workshops. To do this, the coordinators, together with the educators from their centers, filled in the "EVALUATION OF THE INFRASTRUCTURE AND MATERIAL CONDITIONS OF THE TOTAL SCHOOL PROGRAM" (APPENDIX B), also keeping to a scale of 5 to 1, with 5 being the best evaluation, in the proposed items.

Graph 2 shows the result of the evaluation of the number of effective educators for a satisfactory routine at the centers, in the morning and afternoon:

Graph 2 - Number of educators

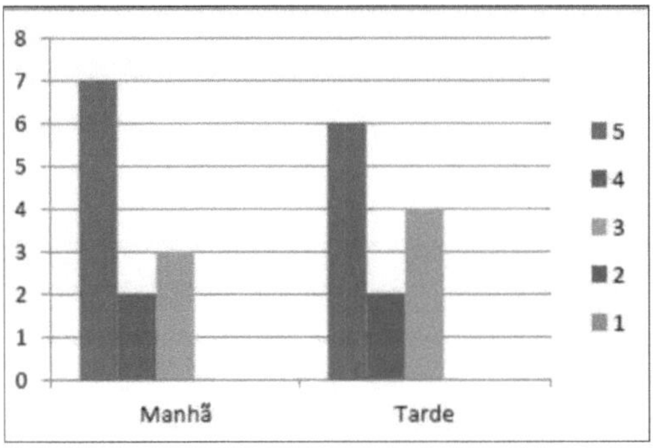

Source: Evaluations provided by the Total School Program (2013/2016).

It is clear from the data presented that there are enough educators to ensure a smooth routine in the centers.

Graph 3 - Furniture

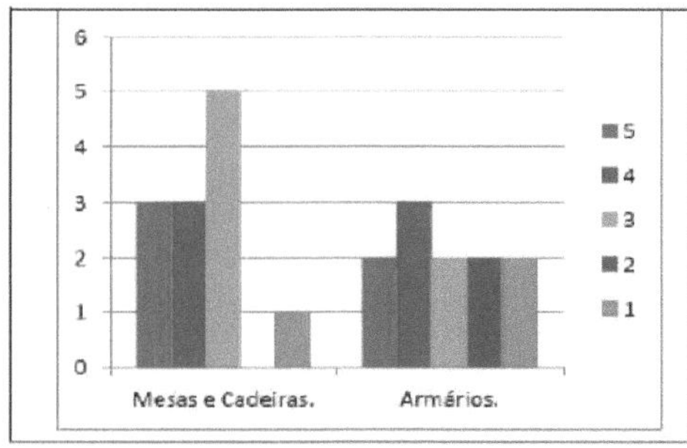

Source: Evaluations provided by the Total School Program (2013/2016).

With regard to the number of tables, chairs and cupboards for the workshops, as shown in Graph 3, we concluded that, in the general picture of the centers, the number is satisfactory, but there is one center that needs more chairs - Parque Roberto Màrio Santini, and four centers that need cupboards: Parque Roberto Màrio Santini, Caruara, Juventude and Marina Magalhaes.

With regard to the materials offered for the work, graph 4, the picture is satisfactory, with a few exceptions.

Graph 4 - Materials offered for the workshops

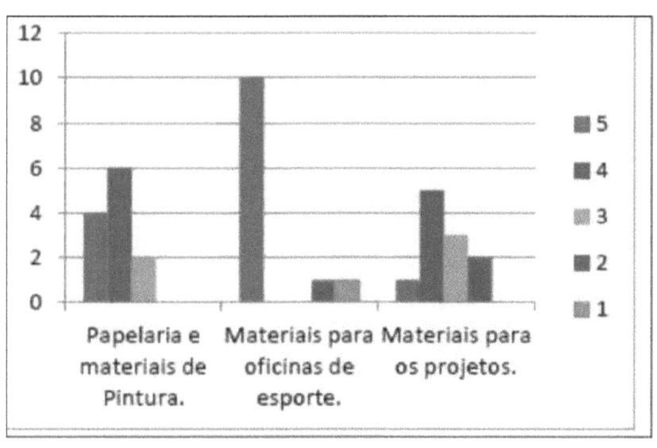

Source: Evaluations provided by the Total School Program (2013/2016).

By analyzing the external and internal environments, we can see that the majority of the service environments are satisfactory, as shown in Graph 5, but we should specifically pay attention to one center with external environment problems: Parque Roberto Màrio Santini (Emissârio/beach), which requests tents to protect the students during the workshops, and two centers with internal environment problems: a) Marina Magalhaes (extension of UME Màrio de Almeida Alcântara), which considers the number of rooms to be insufficient for the service; b) Parque Roberto Màrio Santini, which needs closed rooms.

17

Still on this dimension, the training team, despite not having been mentioned by the center itself, considers that the Rebouças Center also needs to take care of the internal environments, as there is no adequate space for workshops that require a little more concentration from the students, such as Pedagogical Experience/Hour of Duty and Foreign Language.

Graph 5 - Student service environments

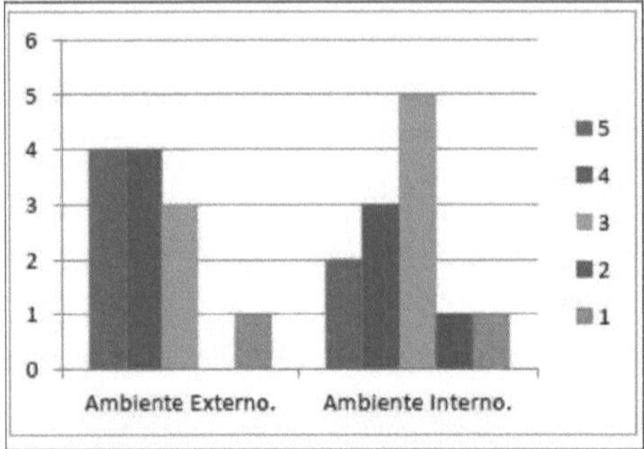

Source: Evaluations provided by the Total School Program (2013/2016).

We found that the infrastructure and material conditions dimension was also satisfactory, with a few exceptions that will have to be improved in subsequent years.

2.4 Dimension: Access and permanence

Students' access to and permanence in comprehensive education are fundamental issues for national education policy (Law 10.172 - National Education Plan). Our municipal policy believes that it is necessary to increase the number of these students, also helping the families of children who are in situations of vulnerability and social risk, especially in areas of the city that do not have cultural, sports and/or leisure facilities.

Currently, students are in the program for approximately 9 hours a day, from Monday to Friday, in full-time Municipal Education Units or in extended hours in the city's service centers.

In 2013, an average of 4,376 students were enrolled, according to Graph 6. It is important to note that, due to the change in municipal management and the entire Total School Program management team in 2013, a detailed process of collecting information on enrollment and attendance only began in April, an action that took place permanently during this administration.

Graph 6 - Students enrolled in the Total School Program

Source: Data provided by the Total School Program (2013).

Looking at the monthly graph, we can see that there is a drop in enrollment in the second semester. We conclude that the coordination team, together with the pedagogical guidance team, need to create strategies every year so that students remain motivated to stay in the program until the end of the school year and/or so that there is greater agility in replacing dropouts with others who want to be enrolled and are on the waiting list.

The data from 2014 to 2016 shows an increase in attendance, but the numbers are lower because the tabulation only includes students enrolled and attending the centers, since the full-time schools were coordinated by subsidized institutions. In 2014, we had 3097 students attending the centers, in 2015 we had a total of 3058 and, in 2016, 3148. The increase in the number of students, despite maintaining the same spaces, is considered by the training team to be a good indicator of the quality of the activities, as we will see in the self-evaluations of the students and parents.

2. 5 Dimension: Educational practices

> The main thing is for each person to have a level of intellectual autonomy that allows them to form their own value judgments in the most varied of situations, and that, in each of these moments, they have the capacity to choose paths and alternatives based on their understanding of reality.
>
> Jacques Delors

According to Article 1 of the Law of Guidelines and Bases of National Education (Law No. 9.394/96), "education encompasses the formative processes that develop in family life, in human coexistence, at work, in educational and research institutions, in social movements and civil society organizations and in cultural manifestations", this article draws society's attention to its educational role.

In reference to formal education, the same law, in its Article 34, encourages education systems to progressively extend the school day in primary education. The school day is considered here as the period in which children and adolescents are under the responsibility of the school, in in-school and/or out-of-school activities. In this way, extending study time or the school day allows for greater integration with other educational spaces that provide diversified educational practices, in an intentional action.

The educational interventions and practices of the extended day need to dialogue with the Pedagogical Political Project of regular education, so that they make more sense and, in their integration, promote the educational and formative character desired of comprehensive care.

As we can see, the school and education professionals embrace the affective, emotional and social dimensions of human development:

> [...] the school recognizes the importance of this approach, understanding that students' development is multidimensional and that learning involves mastering 'non-cognitive' skills of an affective and behavioral nature [...]. (SANTOS; PRIMI, 2014, p. 11)

Broadening the pedagogical horizon beyond the classroom and outside the school walls is not guaranteed simply by extending the length of stay, but by building a new educational paradigm, with a different concept of learning, time and school space.

Therefore, in order to strengthen Integral Education in Santos and with a view to this concept of integral education, the proposal for evaluating and monitoring students' learning was based on the four pillars of education: learning to know, learning to live together, learning to do, as it is understood that this broadens the vision of learning.

The report for Unesco by the International Commission on Education for the 21st Century, Education: a treasure to be discovered, provides a considerable analysis of the development of today's society, the challenges of the process of globalization and modernization, such as coexistence with difference and the need for more peaceful relationships.

Among the reflections, pointers, recommendations and goals, we highlight the discussion on the four pillars of education (learning to know, learning to do, learning to be and learning to live together) and the link with the concept of lifelong education.

Lifelong learning refers to the notion of competence, which is related to dynamic, flexible, collective training. This change stems from the "dematerialization" of work, which requires, in addition to technical skills, the "aptitude for interpersonal relationships" (Delors, 2003, p. 95).

In this way, the monitoring of learning opens up the possibility of reframing activities and building new intervention proposals based on the results obtained, which is extremely important data for the program's training team.

Based on this assumption, an instrument was created to monitor the students' learning (APPENDICES D, E, F and G).

The evaluation was initially carried out on a sample basis (applied to approximately 50% of the students) and the criteria used was to select the centers with the highest number of students enrolled and attending in each of the city's regions, as well as the full-time UMEs in 2013.

A pre-test was carried out, using the four assessment instruments (one for each pillar), in one of the non-participating nuclei of the sample, so that the subsequent application would be successful. We produced a video and written guidelines to unify the application of the assessment.

All educators and coordinators in the Total School Program underwent training to learn about the evaluation tool and how to apply it correctly. The experience was rich and motivating, and the results, analyzed below, reveal the veracity of the information and the seriousness with which the work was carried out in the Program.

We chose to use mandalas in the evaluation of student learning, when we analyzed their use by the Mais Educaçâo Program as a possible strategy for dialogue between knowledge, from the perspective of Integral Education in the face of pedagogical challenges. The Mais Educaçâo Program is an inductive strategy of the Ministry of Education for extending the school day and organizing the curriculum from the perspective of Integral Education.

Why a Mandala? It is the symbol of wholeness (it appears in many primitive and modern cultures) and represents the integration between man and nature. The psychoanalyst and symbol scholar Carl Jung (2000) stated that the Mandala portrays the conditions in which we construct our human experience, between the interior (thought, feeling, intuition and sensation) and the exterior (nature, space and the cosmos), which is in line with the concept of integral education of the Program's coordinators and trainers.

Thus, the mandalas were produced from a reflection on various issues: the training offered to educators (content and strategies), the projects implemented, the standardization of the pedagogical processes created in the Program in 2013 (based on the guidance received during the audit period at the Department of Education, specifically in the Total School Program) and on the research that indicated their functionality.

Therefore, the mandala was characterized as a favorable evaluation tool that allowed the encounter between playfulness and the investigation of the differentiated knowledge built during the year by the students, in a pleasurable, dynamic and creative way in its application.

Figure 1 represents the "learning to do" assessment based on the lessons learned during the year by the Total School Program educators. Based on the instructions given by the assessor, the student had to choose, on a scale of 1 to 5, how much they believed they had learned about what was said in the sentence highlighted in each of the "slices" of the mandala.

Figure 1 - Mandala used as an evaluation tool for "Learning to do".

Source: Evaluations provided by the Total School Program (2013/2016).

Below we present the results obtained in each of the monitored lessons:

2.5.1. LEARNING TO LEARN

Learning to learn advocates stimulating the pleasure of understanding, knowing and discovering. Children and young people need to be encouraged to discover the pleasure of studying. It's worth highlighting the value of curiosity and stimulating students' autonomy, as facilitators in establishing relationships between the content learned and their experiences. We need to think the new, reconstruct the old and reinvent thinking, making the process of understanding, discovering, constructing and reconstructing knowledge a pleasure. Graph 7 shows the results of the evaluation of this learning.

Graph 7 - Learning to learn

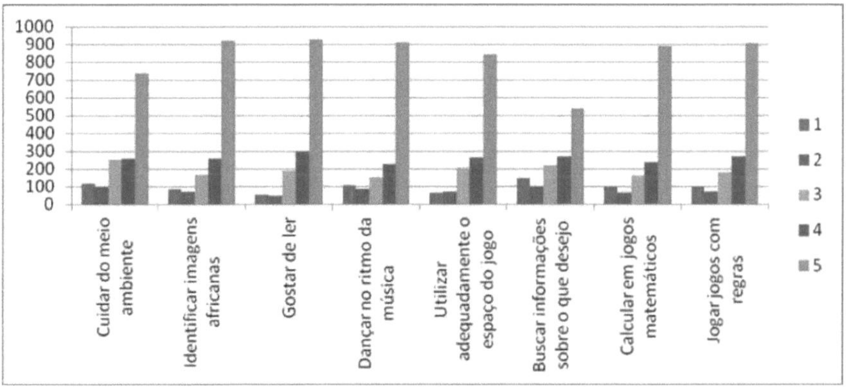

Source: Evaluations provided by the Total School Program (2013/2016).

The evaluation shows us that the learning in this pillar is quite satisfactory and that enjoying reading, playing and dancing are activities that are present in the daily lives of the children and young people taking part in the program.

Another point that should be emphasized is that care for the environment needs to be worked on more and that the majority have not yet learned to look for information about what they want, in other words, the investigative spirit and research skills need to be looked at more carefully.

2.5.2 LEARNING TO LIVE TOGETHER

Knowing how to live together is one of the great challenges of this century, when humanity is marked by wars and conflicts. In education, we hope to encourage ethical coexistence between different groups and enable conflicts to be resolved peacefully, assuming the dimension of being human, as interdependent beings.

Graph 8 - Learning to get along

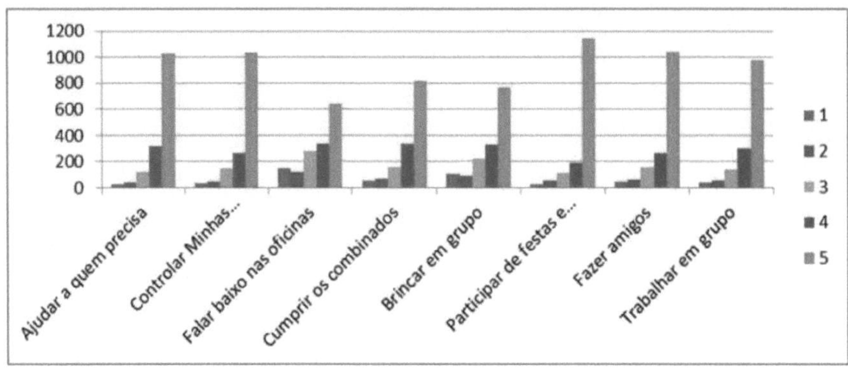

Source: Evaluations provided by the Total School Program (2013/2016).

The evaluation of the "socializing" pillar reflects the daily life of the centers, as shown in graph 8, in which most of the students participate adequately in parties, make friends, help those in need, but there is difficulty in keeping to agreements and speaking quietly in workshops/activities, which hinders or makes it impossible to work together with quality. We verified the sincerity of the students and the accuracy of the data, which translates into numbers the reality monitored by the trainers during their visits, in contact with the centers, educators and students.

2.5.3 LEARNING TO DO

Related to the skill of execution, "doing" is closely related to "knowing". It is therefore necessary to provide practical activities for students to put what they know into play in order to carry out the tasks.

Another point worth remembering is that "doing" usually takes place collectively or in small groups and it becomes essential to resolve conflicts, to have the initiative and flexibility to carry out what has been requested, encouraging the courage to take risks, to make mistakes without fear of getting it right, in short, the ability to do and cooperate.

Graph 9 - Learning to do

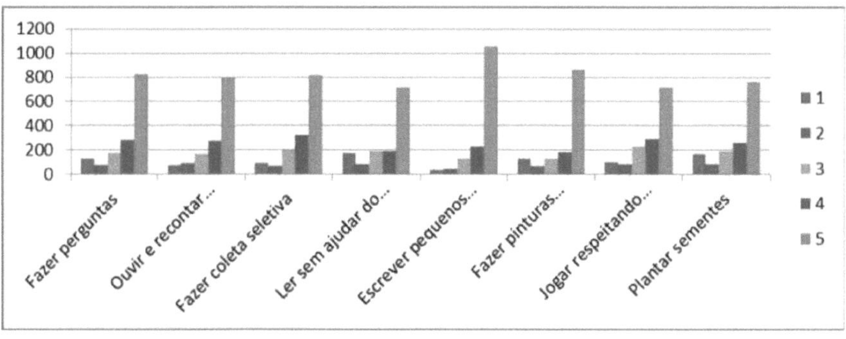

Source: Evaluations provided by the Total School Program (2013/2016).

According to graph 9, the "learning to do" analyses generated several questions about the reading and writing process. A significant number of students (1,055) said they had learned to write short texts with a lot of skill (score 5) and, on the other hand, the lowest score of 5 was for reading without help (715), i.e. autonomy in reading and writing.

Reading still needs a lot of intervention and is far removed from the students' daily lives. With regard to the work with the Africanity project, it can be seen that in several pillars it appears as something that favored learning, as well as the work with "storytelling", "the ability to ask questions" and "separating garbage for selective collection".

2.5.4 LEARNING TO BE

This pillar reaffirms the concept of education in a comprehensive and integral way, investing in the biopsychosocial formation of the human being. Learning to be involves autonomy and discovering one's own potential for fulfillment, in a consumerist and materialistic society in which it is necessary to awaken students to the dimensions of personal and community fulfillment, in other words, learning needs to be integral, considering all the individual's potential.

Graph 10 - Learning to be

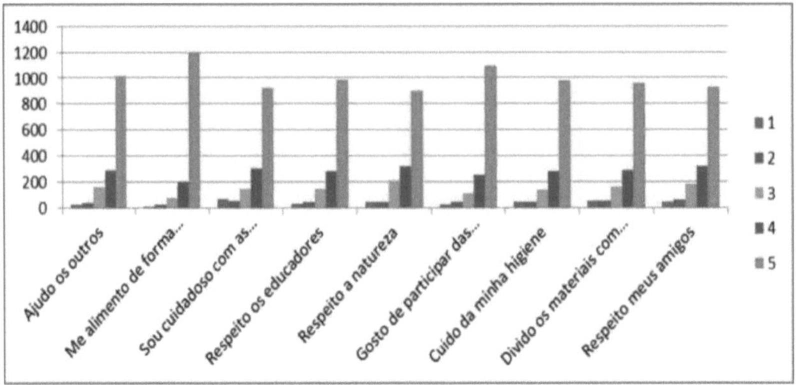

Source: Evaluations provided by the Total School Program (2013/2016).

The result, shown in graph 10, shows that the "learning to be" pillar is being worked on in a balanced and efficient way. It also makes us reflect on the development of students who are much more open to showing their true feelings, helping without expecting a return and caring for others more spontaneously than adults, who may or may not have experienced situations that prevent them from dedicating themselves to others so naturally.

The item that stood out the most was healthy eating, which draws attention to the fact that the students in the comprehensive education program eat most of their meals at the UME/Program, with menus and snacks prepared/guided by nutritionists. In this way, we can see that the students identify healthy eating and the various possibilities for practicing harmonious coexistence with their classmates.

2.6 PARENT AND GUARDIAN SATISFACTION SURVEY

Comprehensive Education also promotes closer ties between students and their families, creating mechanisms that help strengthen bonds by motivating students and their families to take part in events and projects throughout the year. Generally, these are shows of work in which the students are placed in the spotlight, through projects, presentations or championships and festivals. These practices value the student and improve their self-esteem, which is reflected in their family life, as parents feel proud of their children, forming a virtuous circle of love and appreciation for the family.

Therefore, considering the opinion of family members in the evaluation process strengthens the family as a unit of reference for the students, strengthens links with the Comprehensive Education Program and makes it possible to share responsibility for the education of children and adolescents, often from families with social risks and reduced cultural possibilities.All those responsible for the students participating in the

26

Comprehensive Education Program were sent a questionnaire to fill in voluntarily (APPENDIX C). We then analyzed the return of 1384 questionnaires (34%), a positive rate considering that it was a voluntary document.

A survey carried out by the Datafolha Institute (19/09/2013) with teenage students, requested by Itaù Social (Available at:<

http://g1.globo.com/educacao/noticia/2013/09/23-dos-alunos-acham-que-educacao-integral-evita-violencia-diz-   pesquisa.html, found that 23% of students aged 16 and over think that comprehensive education is a way of preventing crime, violence and drug use and reveals that 90% of those interviewed think that comprehensive education is necessary for the future of the new generations.

With the data collected in surveys like the one above and the information gathered from the parents of students participating in the program, we cross-checked the information collected with the parameters established and based on these elements we found some similarities that we will detail below.

Data analysis reveals the satisfaction of those responsible for the care offered.

With regard to interest in the program, 99% of those responsible, see graph 11, said that their child shows interest in the activities and the few who don't indicate a lack of willingness on the part of the student or a lack of commentary at home.

Graph 11 - Students' interest in Total School Program activities

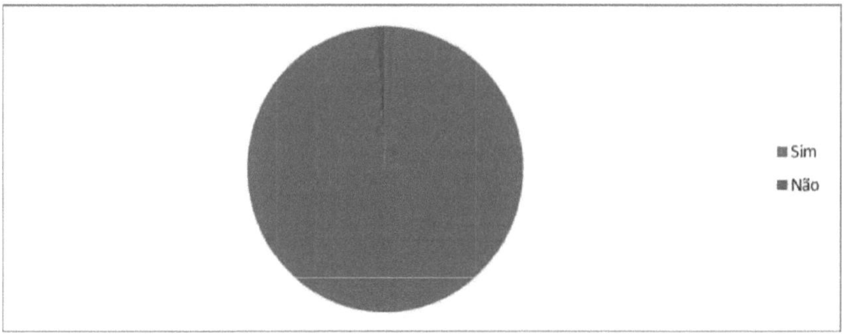

Source: Evaluations provided by the Total School Program (2013/2016).

With regard to what the student most enjoys doing in the Program, graph 12, the vast majority, almost 50% of respondents, said that sport was the most enjoyable of the various activities on offer.

Graph 12 - Activity that the student enjoys most in the Program

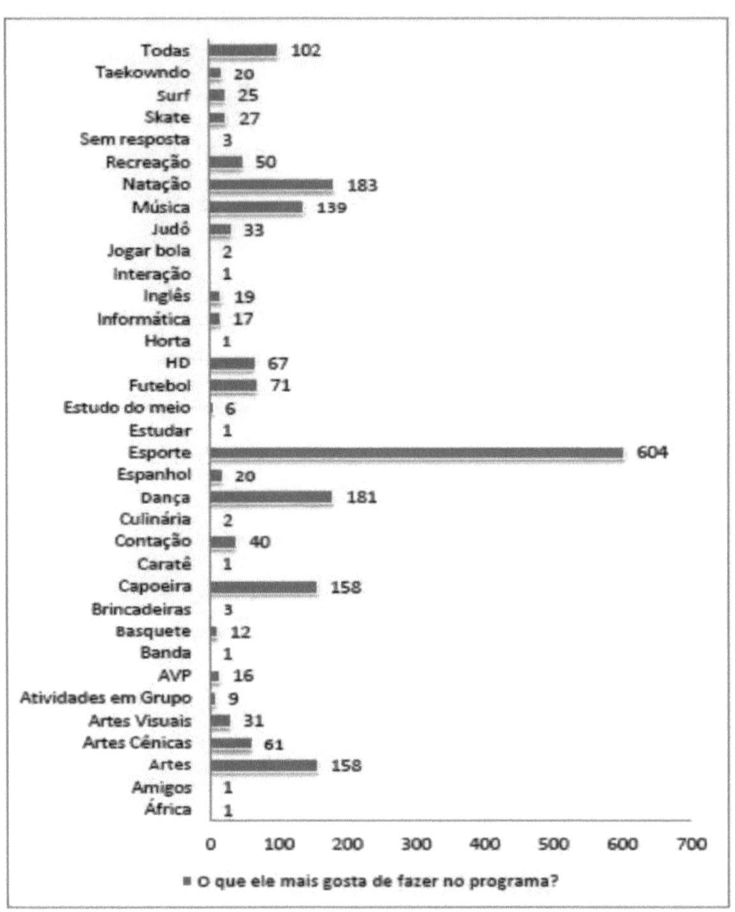

Source: Evaluations provided by the Total School Program (2013/2016).

It is important to note that the questionnaire sent to those responsible is also made up of subjective (open-ended) questions, in which those responsible answer, in the same question, several items that reflect their position. These answers were then categorized.

Looking at graph 12, we can see that several modalities within the arts axis were flagged (visual arts, performing arts, arts, Africa, dance, music). Skateboarding and surfing, which are responsible for maintaining and attracting many young people to the program, also had a minimal evaluation due to the fact that the activity is only offered to students aged 10 and over, and only in a few centers. The workshops on offer are very varied, meaning that the centers don't have the same workshops, which was taken into account during the analysis.

The interpretation of the data also occurs with other workshops that are present in only a few centers due to the difficulty of finding an educator with specific training or adequate space in the centers, such as the photography workshop. Another surprise was the evaluation of swimming, with 183 nominations and offered in only three centers, meaning that practically all the parents who have children from these centers listed swimming as their students' preferred activity.

When asked what the child or adolescent would be interested in learning more about through the activities offered by the Program, dance, music, sport and art stood out, but there was a fairly even balance between the various workshops selected, as can be seen in graph 13.

Graph 13 - Student interest in learning more about something developed by the Program

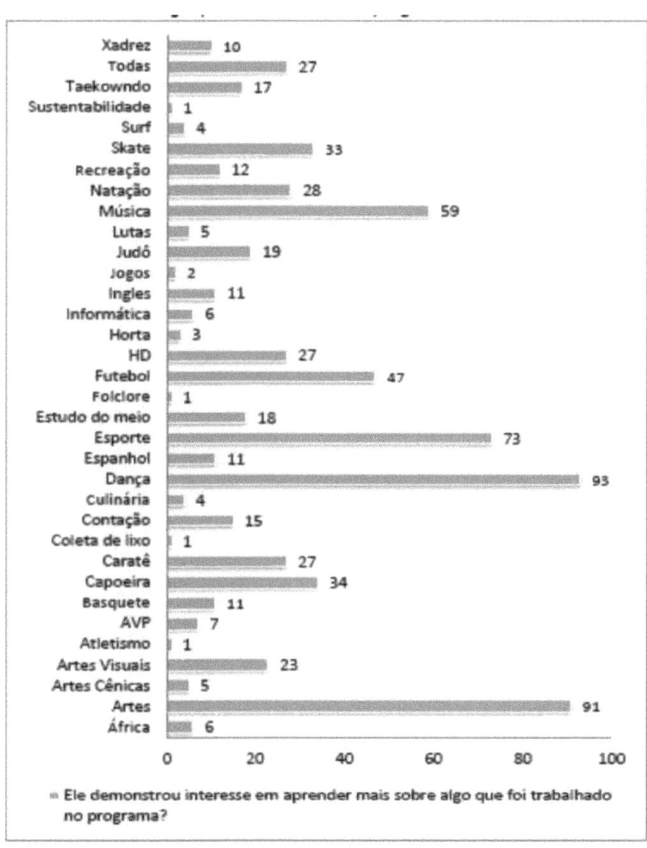

Source: Evaluations provided by the Total School Program (2013/2016).

When it comes to what students say at home about what they do in the program, Graph 14 shows that more than 95% of students talk to their parents about what they do. The act of talking at home about the activities carried out in the centers fosters a dialogical relationship between parents and children, which for the program is a positive indicator of quality.

Graph 14 - Does the student comment on what they do in the Total School program?

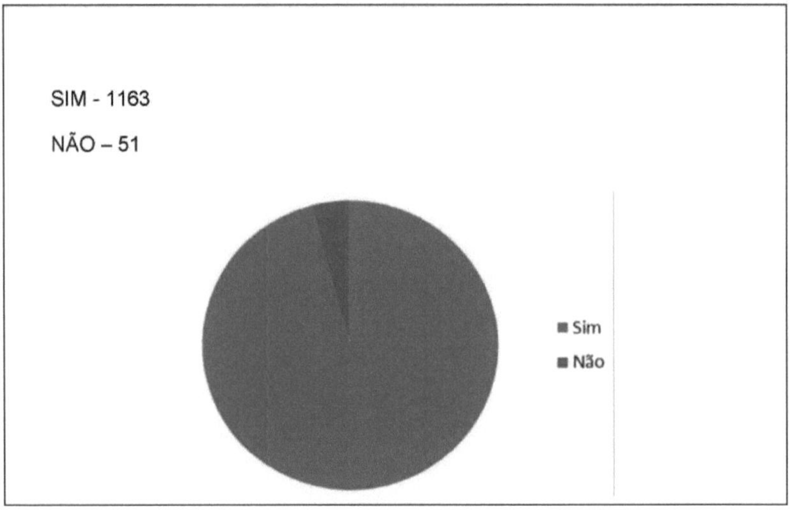

Source: Evaluations provided by the Total School Program (2013/2016).

We understand that the work to encourage greater family involvement with their children is still incipient in the Program's daily routine. The work proposed by the Program, aimed at working more closely with the family, with a view to increasing their capacity for dialogue and a relationship of trust with their children and adolescents, needs other strategies in order to be effective and lead to reflections on the responsibility of parents in relation to their students' education.

Parent orientation meetings were held in partnership with some Municipal Education Units, where it was observed that there was a need to invest in this dialogue as a way of enhancing the protagonism of families in a reflective and non-assistance way, through welcoming and personal empowerment.

With regard to the reason why parents enroll their children in the Comprehensive Education Program, graph 15, open and subjective question, it is important to note that the same answer often contained several reasons.

The analysis revealed that the main reason is to leave their children in a safe place, which demonstrates the parents' confidence in the program. Other reasons were highlighted, such as: to improve development, the diversity of activities, because the students like it, because they learn new things, because of the extracurricular activities.

Graph 15 - Parents' reason for enrolling in the program

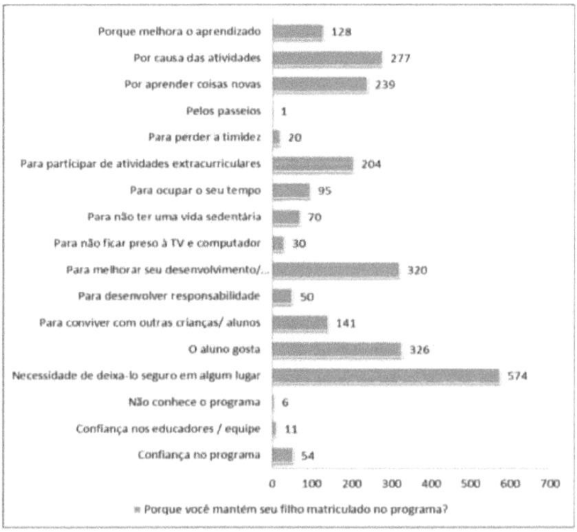

Source: Evaluations provided by the Total School Program (2013/2016).

In the light of the above, it can be seen that the welfare aspect, which is often pointed out, is irrelevant, since the quality of the activities is of equal importance to parents choosing where to leave their children.

To conclude the analysis of the graph above, we consider the parents' evaluation to be very positive and the results have generated recommendations to help overcome the difficulties inherent in situations of social vulnerability and the intergenerational cycle of poverty, valuing community knowledge that represents the local cultural universe, what our students bring to school and to the nuclei and, at the same time, expanding the opportunities for constant learning.

3 Reflections on evaluation and monitoring

Reflecting during the journey is like planning a trip and stepping back at times to appreciate the landscape from different angles. The vision that implies the need to distance oneself in order to analyze the path taken is directly related to the proposal to evaluate, self-evaluate and monitor.

The weaknesses exposed in the evaluations carried out at different levels (students, parents, coordinators) allowed us to take a closer look at the socio-educational process involved in the Comprehensive Education proposal.

The idea of using different spaces for the hubs in which the activities of extending the working day are carried out makes it possible to understand that each of the scenarios involved implies different forms of connection with the culture and logic of community participation. As Jaqueline Moll and Gesuina Leclerc point out:

> Education policy must be linked to a broad network of social and cultural policies, social actors and public facilities. Therein lies the importance of considering policies for an educating municipality, articulating the relationships between the municipality, the community, the school and the different educational agents, so that the city itself becomes an educational agent. (LECLERC; MOLL, 2010, p. 54)

Leaving the school also implies leaving the pre-established and finding new ways of moving in search of meaningful learning and experiences.

In search of this movement, after using the same assessment tool (mandalas) for three consecutive years, we realized the need to adapt the assessments.

It is worth noting that the students' assessments have always followed the principle of self-assessment, which according to Perrenoud (1999) is not about multiplying external feedback, but about training students to regulate their own thinking and learning processes.

The challenge intrinsic to the development of a new self-assessment tool for students was to maintain the principles that underpin Integral Education in the Program, the Four Pillars of Education, and to avoid the segregation between the principles portrayed in different mandalas.

Another aspect incorporated into the new model concerns the use of technology, a language close to the universe of children and adolescents.

We came up with the idea of using a self-assessment in the form of a digital traffic light, following the traffic light rules in which red would represent non-learning; yellow, partially learned content and concepts; and green, satisfactory learning.

Two self-assessment instruments were drawn up, the first for classes T1 and T2, students aged between 6 and 10, and the second for classes T3 and T4, made up of students aged between 11 and 14.

The statement read: "To answer the questions below, use the idea of a traffic light. Click on red if you think you haven't learned enough, yellow if you need to learn a bit more and click on green when you think you've learned enough."

The questions were then presented with the traffic light, as shown in the image below:

Trabalho em grupo e colaboro com os amigos

Opção 1

Opção 2

Opção 3

The community educators who took part in applying the assessments reported that the participating students appreciated the new self-assessment format, mainly because of the use of technology, since they answered directly via the educators' smartphones.

Another extremely important aspect concerns the tabulation of data, which in the *online* format used in the Google form, reveals the results immediately after the respondent sends in the completed form.

Below is an example of two questions automatically tabulated, with the number of respondents (1484, in the evaluations of classes T1 and T2), at the top of the form.

Trabalho em grupo e colaboro com os amigos
1.482 respostas

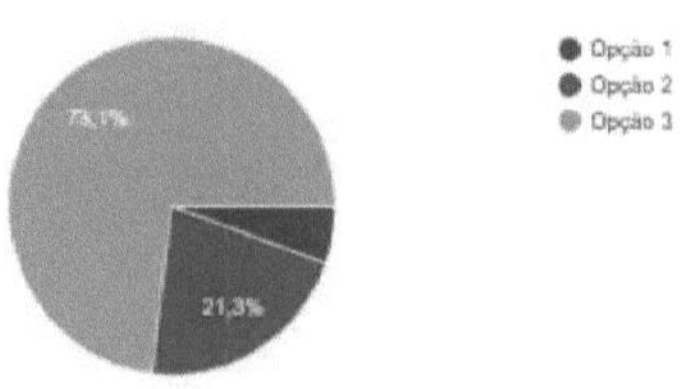

Eu aprendi a ouvir o outro com atenção e respeitar sua opinião
1.482 respostas

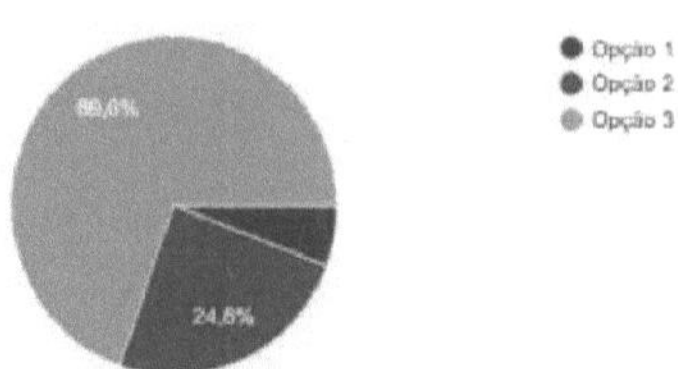

The reports from educators, coordinators and students were highly stimulating for continuing the research in search of meaningful, challenging and coherent activities for today's students.

Allowing the different pillars of education to talk to each other while avoiding segregation reinforces the concept of integrality, which must be present in the concept, in the proposals for activities and when evaluating knowledge and the Program in general. To support the vision of integrality between the pillars, we used Delors himself, when he said that "learning to know and learning to do are, to a large extent, inseparable" (DELORS, 1998, p. 93).

FINAL CONSIDERATIONS

In the course of this work, it is possible to understand the relationship between the evaluation process, the discourse of Full-Time Education and the educational policies that are articulated at municipal level.

While acknowledging other points in the aforementioned research that relate to the concept of Integral Education, this work prioritized discussions of the four pillars of education and the concept of Integral Education in an experience in the sphere of municipal public education in order to achieve the proposed reflection.

The research presented here has proved to be an important tool in guiding ways to improve the quality of care for students participating in the Total School Program.

The results of this evaluation, in the five dimensions indicated by this study, make it possible to improve the Program by focusing on the needs presented, the weaknesses and potentialities revealed in the course of the study.

In general, we believe that the Program achieved its objectives satisfactorily between 2013 and 2016, but when it comes to quality in education, we know that the pursuit of excellence must be the goal of public policies.

Therefore, we understand that the evaluation and monitoring of the Program must be continuous in order to make practical recommendations and set increasingly effective and efficient goals in the care of the children and adolescents served by the Program.

However, it is clear that these are broad relationships that still need to be reflected on, conceiving the interfaces between education and society. To ignore the needs of today's society and the challenges of working in Full-Time Education would be to invalidate the data and allow the existing situation to continue without reflection and co-responsibility for the changes that are still needed to serve all students who have the right to Full-Time Education.

Finally, we would like to point out that we do not allow the naturalized discourse of parents and the community who believe that they are receiving assistance because they have nowhere to leave their children during the day. We would like to make it clear that comprehensive education is a right provided for in the Brazilian Constitution and that understanding the possibility of social transformation promoted by education is what is done by recognizing the history built by individuals. It is necessary to unveil and strengthen the relationships within them and seek coherence between the words and actions that are practiced on a daily basis in contact with the real agents of transformation in Brazilian society.

BIBLIOGRAPHICAL REFERENCES

ARENDT, Hanna. **The crisis in education.** In: Between the past and the future. Sao Paulo: Perspectiva, 1979.

ARROYO, M. **Broken images. Trajectories and times of students and teachers.** Petrópolis, RJ: Vozes, 2004.

Caderno Rede de Saberes - Mais Educaçâo. Available at: http://portal.mec.gov.br/index.php?option=com content&view=article&id=16727&Itemid=1119 Accessed on October 15, 2017.

CAVALIERE, Ana Maria. **Integral education.** In: OLIVEIRA, Dalila Andrade et al. Dicionârio trabalho, profissâo e condiçâo docente. Belo Horizonte: UFMG/Faculty of Education, 2010. CD ROM.

DELORS, Jacques and EUFRAZIO, José Carlos. **Education: a treasure to discover.** Sâo Paulo: Cortez, 1998.

FREIRE, P. **Pedagogia da Autonomia - Saberes necessàrios à pràtica educativa.** Sâo Paulo: Paz e Terra, 1987.

. **Pedagogy of the oppressed.** Rio de Janeiro: Paz e Terra, 1991.

FREITAS, L. C. **Avaliaçâo: construindo o campo e a critica.** Florianópolis: Insular, 2002.

JUNG, Carl Gustav. **Archetypes and the Collective Unconscious.** Petrópolis : Vozes, 2000. Chapter XII - The symbolism of mandalas.

LECLERC, Gesuina de F. E. ; MOLL, Jaqueline (Org.). **Politicas de educaçâo integral em jornada ampliada.** Em Aberto, Brasilia, v. 25, n. 88, p. 1-214, jul./dez. 2012.

MATURANA, H. **Emotions and Language in Education and Politics.** Belo Horizonte: Editora UFMG, 1998.

MOLL, Jaqueline; LECLERC, Gesuina. **Integral and community education: taking leave of the city and the school.** In: Padilha, Paulo; Ceccon, Sheila; RamalhO, Priscila. Municipio que educa: mùltiplos olhares. Sao Paulo: Paulo Freire Institute, 2010.

MOLL, J. **Juventude, cidade e espaços de convivência e aprendizagem: novos olhares.** Lecture given at the Seminar: School without walls - a new geography of learning. LEARNING SCHOOL CITY. Sao Paulo,   September 28th, 2005. 2005. Available http://aprendiz.uol.com.br/downloads/educacao comunitaria/trilhas.doc

. **Life stories, school stories: elements for a pedagogy of the city**. Petrópolis: Vozes, 2000. 48 Em Aberto, Brasilia, v. 25, n. 88, p. 17-49, jul./dez. 2012.

. **Full-time schools**. In: OLIVEIRA, Dalila Andrade et al. Dicionàrio trabalho, profissâo e condiçâo docente. Belo Horizonte: UFMG/Faculty of Education, 2010. 1 CD ROM.

PARO, Vitor H. **Educação integral em tempo integral: uma concepçâo de educação para a modernidade**. In: COELHO, Ligia M. C. da Costa (Org.). Educação integral em tempo integral: estudos e experiência em processo. Petrópolis, RJ: DP et Alii; Rio de Janeiro: Faperj, 2009.

PATTO, M.H.S. **Para uma critica da razâo psicométrica**. Psychol. USP, v. 8, n. 1, Sâo Paulo, p. 47-62, 1997. Available at <http://dx.doi.org/10.1590/S0103-65641997000100004>. Accessed on: 14 Nov. 2016.

PERRENOUD, P. **Evaluation: from excellence to the regulation of learning - between two logics**. Trad. Patricia Chittoni Ramos. Porto Alegre: Artes Médicas Sul, 1999.

SANTOS, M. **The Nature of Space: Technique and Time, Reason and Emotion**. São Paulo, Hucitec, 1996.

SANTOS, D.; PRIMI, R. **Socio-emotional development and school learning: a measurement proposal to support public policies**. Report on the preliminary results of the project to measure socio-emotional competencies in Rio de Janeiro. Sâo Paulo: OECD, sEeDUC, Ayrton Senna Institute, 2014.

APPENDICES

APPENDIX A - EVALUATION OF "EDUCATOR TRAINING"

PUBLIC: CORE COORDINATORS

1. To evaluate the training of general education teachers at the Coonjaiado Center this year, put an X_1 on a scale of 5 to 1 (5 being the best evaluation). in the following aspects:

	5	4	3	2	1
number of training meetings					
b)Use of what was oriented in the formations and what was carried out in the nucleus					
c Viability of the Suggested Projects (Africanity and SustainabilityJ					
dj Greater interest among students in the workshops					
e) Trainers visit their Nùcleo for guidance > the general jxil io					

For the items you rated less than B_1 lifiq je jus your answer, recording more details:

Note: It is not necessary to identify yourself.

APPENDIX B - EVALUATION OF THE "INFRASTRUCTURE AND MATERIAL CONDITIONS" OF THE TOTAL SCHOOL PROGRAM

PUBLIC: NÙCLE COORDEMADERS

Name of the Coonderadon_______________________________________

N udeo : ____

Evaluate the overall structure of the Coordinated Center you have been involved in this year, by placing an X on a scale of 5 to 1 (5 being the best evaluation), in the following aspects:

		5	4	3	2	1
a) Materials offered for the workshops.	a.1. Stationery and painting materials.					
	a.2. Materials for the spore workshops.					
	a.3. Materials for the projects.					
bj Mobiliano.	b.1. Tables and chairs.					
	b.2 Arnnarios.					
c) Physical space of the center.	c.1. external environment.					

	c.2 Internal environment.					
d) Number of educators to satisfactory retina.	d.1. morning.					
	d.2 Afternoon.					

For the items you evaluated out of 3, justify your answer by recording the main details of the requirements:

APPENDIX C - Parent/Caregiver Evaluation

PARENTS / GUARDIAN

Name of person responsible: ____

Student: _________________________________ **Year:** ______________

UME: ____

Core: ____

1. Regarding your child's participation in the TOTAL SCHOOL PROGRAM, please answer the questions below:

a. Is he/she interested in the activities of the TOTAL SCHOOL PROGRAM ?

( ) yes ( ) no, why

b. What does he/she like most about the PROGRAM?

c. Did he/she show an interest in learning more about something that was worked on in the PROGRAM?

d. Does he/she take what he/she has learned into conversations at home, comment on what he/she does in the PROGRAM?

( ) always ( ) almost always ( ) occasionally ( ) never

2. why do you keep your child enrolled in the program?

Aprender a Ser

respeito meus amigos.
ajudo os outros.
me alimento de forma saudável.
sou cuidadoso com as coisas.
respeito os educadores
respeito a natureza.
gosto de participar das atividades.
cuido da minha higiene.
divido os materiais com meus amigos.
Eu

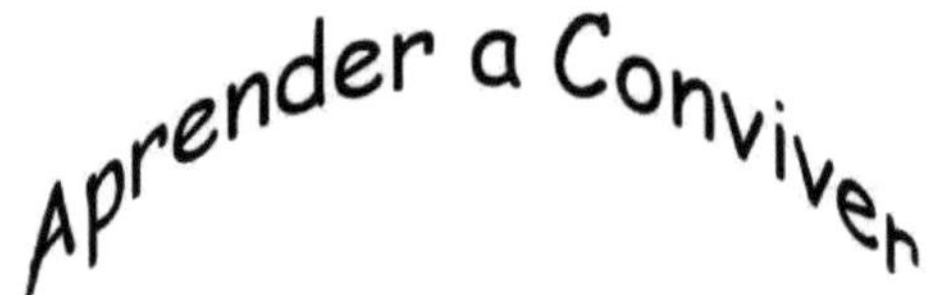
Aprender a Conviver

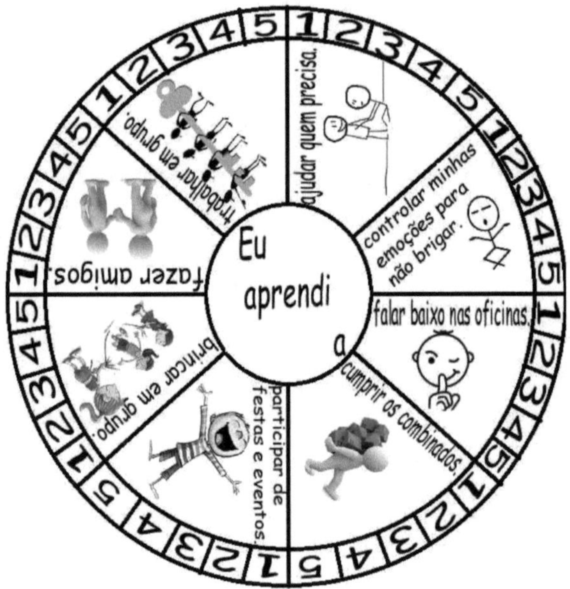
Eu aprendi a
ajudar quem precisa.
controlar minhas emoções para não brigar.
falar baixo nas oficinas.
cumprir os combinados.
participar de festas e eventos.
brincar em grupo.
fazer amigos.
trabalhar em grupo.
1 2 3 4 5

Aprender a Fazer
Eu aprendi a
fazer perguntas
ouvir e recontar histórias.
fazer coleta seletiva.
ler sem ajuda do educador.
escrever pequenos textos
fazer pinturas africanas
jogar respeitando as regras.
plantar sementes.

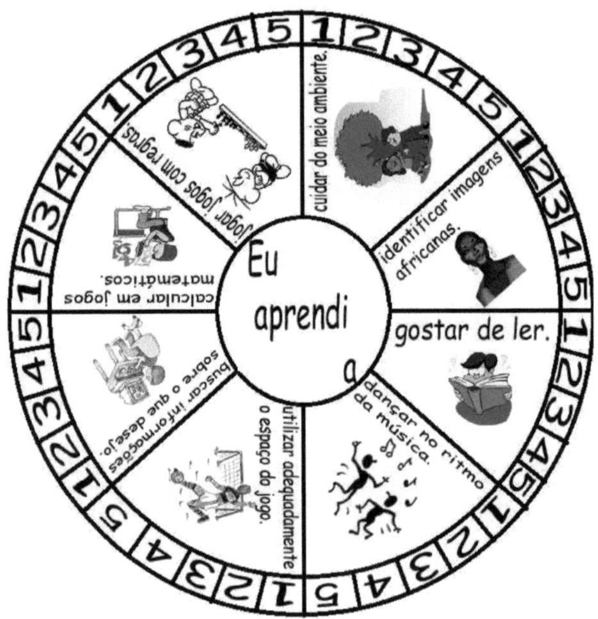

APPENDIX H - Letter to parents

LETTER TO PARENTS

Parents,

It is with great satisfaction that we begin our contact with you and your children.

In 2013, we will have a new way of coordinating the program, with a pedagogical guidance team that aims to offer didactic support to the professionals who are part of the program.

In order to guarantee better service for our students, we will be holding monthly training sessions and courses with the educators. The meetings will take place on the first Friday of every month (except public holidays) during working hours. We are counting on your understanding because, on this day, students will not have full-day classes, only regular classes.

The scheduled dates are April 4, May 3, June 7, August 2, September 6 and November 8.

We are giving you advance notice so that you have time to organize your routine with your children and thus help us to improve the quality of our service.

We thank you for your trust and count on your cooperation.

Educational Guidance Team

APPENDIX I - *Online* evaluation template

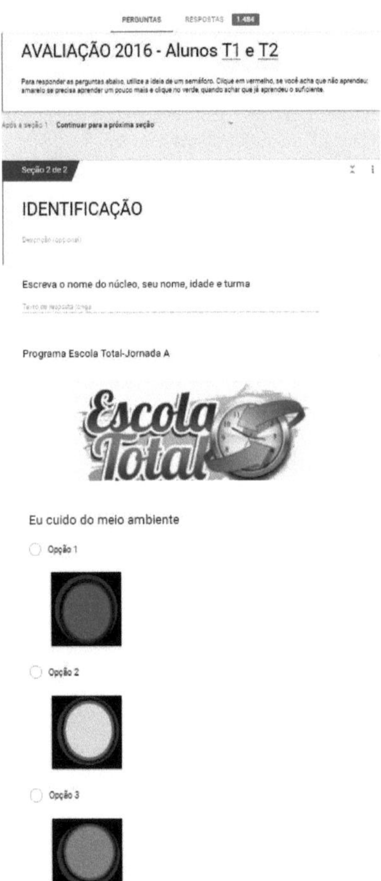

Note: All the other questions follow the same format as the traffic light so that students can click on the answer they most identify with.